GHOST
WATCH

A Play by Jon Blake

Series Editors: Steve Barlow and Steve Skidmore

Heinemann

Published by Heinemann Educational Publishers
Halley Court, Jordan Hill, Oxford OX2 8EJ
A division of Reed Educational and Professional Publishing Ltd

OXFORD   MELBOURNE   AUCKLAND
JOHANNESBURG   BLANTYRE   GABORONE
IBADAN   PORTSMOUTH NH (USA)   CHICAGO

First published 2001
05 04 03 02 01
10   9   8   7   6   5   4   3   2   1
ISBN 0 435 21450 0

Illustrations by Andrew Skilleter
Cover Design by Shireen Nathoo Design
Cover artwork by Andrew Skilleter
Designed by Artistix, Thame, Oxon
Printed and bound in Great Britain by Biddles Ltd

Tel: 01865 888058 www.heinemann.co.uk

Contents

Characters

Fish is a cocky lad, who likes to show off and play the boss.

Coop is a bit of a 'mummy's boy', less brave than Fish, but capable of holding his own in banter.

Marko is the joker of the bunch. He is popular, and rather more thoughtful than the others.

Gasman is the outsider, and afraid to join in the laddish games. He is the butt of the other boys' jokes – but he's looking to get his revenge.

SCENE ONE

A farmer's field on a cliff top, with two small tents in it. Evening.
Fish and Coop are lying cramped inside one of the tents, one up,
one down. Fish has a video camera and binoculars, and he is looking
out of the tent towards a barn across the field. Marko and Gasman
are in the other tent, nearby.

COOP: Fish, will you get your feet out of my face?

FISH: I'm doing the video diary.

COOP: Well, do it down this end!

FISH: You come down this end!

COOP: You're polluting the pillows.

FISH: Just shut up moaning, will you? You've been moaning since day one!

COOP: This is day one.

FISH: Yeah, and you've been moaning all through it. *(Moaning)* 'My mum will kill me if I get wet!'

COOP: Well, she will! If anything goes wrong, I'm grounded.

FISH: Your mum's a dragon.

COOP: Shut up!

FISH: She even tells you off for sneezing!

COOP: Don't talk about it, right?

FISH: Well, stop moaning then. *(Switches on video)* Day one. Coop and Fish have set up base camp in a field beside Nash Cliff. Marko is in tent two with – yuk – Gasman.

COOP: Tough luck, Marko.

FISH: Ssh! Bishop's Farm is just the other side of the fence. We can see the Red Barn clearly. No sign yet of the ghost of Lady Jasper. But wait, what's this? *(He knocks over a carton of milk. Loudly)* Aaaaaargh!

COOP: Fish, you idiot, you've knocked over the milk!

FISH: You shouldn't have put it there!

COOP: It's all over my spare pants!

FISH: Here, I'll wipe it up.

COOP: That's my spare T-shirt!

(Marko appears at the tent door.)

MARKO: Who screamed?

COOP: That idiot! He's knocked over the milk.

MARKO: Oh no! I can't eat Sugar Puffs without milk!

FISH: You're always thinking of your stomach, you are.

MARKO: Better than thinking of Gasman's.

COOP: Been trumping, has he?

MARKO: I'd rather share a tent with a pig.

FISH: Tough luck. You lost the toss.

MARKO: Can't we just send him home?

COOP: Yeah, if he didn't own the tents.

MARKO: Let us in, then.

FISH: No!

MARKO: I'll tell you a joke.

FISH: Go on, then.

MARKO: Man goes to the doctor's, right, and says, 'Doctor, there's a strawberry growing out of my belly button.' Doctor takes a look and says, 'You want to put some cream on that.'

(The others laugh.)

FISH: Okay. You can come in for five minutes. Five minutes, right.

MARKO: You're a mate, Fish.

(Marko crams himself inside.)

COOP: You been watching the barn?

MARKO: Gasman has. He won't let me have the binoculars.

FISH: We don't need the binoculars. She's coming right by us.

MARKO: *(Sticking his head outside)* Where?

FISH: Not now, you div! I mean she *will* come right by us.

COOP: Midnight.

FISH: She drifts across the field, with her baby in her arms, and vanishes over the cliff.

(Pause.)

MARKO: What if the video don't pick her up?

COOP: Why shouldn't it?

MARKO: Ghosts don't come out on photos.

FISH: No! It's the other way round! They're invisible, then they come out on photos.

MARKO: If she's invisible, how do we know she's there?

FISH: They're not all invisible. Anyway, there's a freaky chill when she passes ... and a smell of rotting flesh.

MARKO: That ain't Lady Jasper! That's Gasman!

(Others laugh. The tent door parts to reveal Gasman.)

GASMAN: Did I hear my name?

(Others groan.)

COOP: Get lost, Gasman!

FISH: No room in here.

GASMAN: I'm bored.

COOP: Tough.

GASMAN: It's my tent.

FISH: Tough.

MARKO: Oh, come on, boys. It is his tent.

COOP: Okay. You can come in if you tell a joke.

GASMAN: All right. *(Pause)* There's an ice-cream man and he's dead in his van, covered in chopped nuts. Did himself in.

FISH: Uh?

MARKO: Topped himself, you idiot!

GASMAN: Oh yeah – topped himself.

          (Others groan.)

COOP: You told it wrong, you div!

GASMAN: So? It's still a joke.

FISH: You're a joke.

          (Gasman forces himself in.)

FISH: Just keep a cork in it, Gasman.

MARKO: We're short of oxygen, as it is.

COOP: He can't help it. It's cos he's so scared.

GASMAN: Am not.

COOP: Yes, you are. That's why you've come in here. You're scared of anything, you are.

FISH: Hey, remember when we were on the footbridge?

GASMAN: Oh, shut up.

FISH: Jamie goes over the edge and starts climbing along the outside. So I get up on the handrail and start walking down there. Then we look at Gasman, and he's clutching his leg. 'Pulled a muscle!' he says.

GASMAN: I had pulled a muscle!

FISH: You were just scared to do anything dangerous!

(The others jeer at Gasman.)

GASMAN: Oh yeah? What about you in Pound World?

FISH: What?

GASMAN: Fish sees this sign: EVERYTHING £1. So he goes up to the girl on the till and says, 'Does that include you?' And she just looks at him, then points to the other sign: ALL CHILDREN MUST BE ACCOMPANIED BY AN ADULT.

(The others laugh.)

COOP: Ah, wicked! *(Pause)* What's the time? I'm getting fed up waiting for this ghost. *(He picks up the video camera and points it at the barn.)*

MARKO: Who was this Lady Jasper, anyhow?

FISH: *(To Marko)* Here, give us that torch. *(Fish takes the torch and shines it under his chin to sinister effect)* Lady Jasper. Wife of the sinister Lord Jasper. Bore him a child.

COOP: Oh yeah?

FISH: But the kid was dark-skinned – it wasn't Lord Jasper's! When Lord Jasper saw it, he seized it from her and, in a fit of rage, smothered it under a pillow.

COOP: Cushion.

FISH: *(Irritated)* Cushion, then! Anyway, when she saw what he'd done, she buried the baby in the barn.

GASMAN: Oo-er!

COOP : Yeah, and they say, if she touches you, you become one of them – the undead!

GASMAN: *(Sarcastic)* Yeah, right.

FISH: It's true!

GASMAN: *(Suddenly jumps)* Hey, get off, Marko, you weirdo!

MARKO: What?

GASMAN: You touched my arm, you weirdo! Get off!

MARKO: I never touched you!

GASMAN: Did!

MARKO: Did not!

GASMAN: I felt your cold fingers!

MARKO: I'm wearing gloves.

(Pause.)

GASMAN: What touched me, then?

(All jump up, yelling in panic. A mobile phone rings, creating more chaos. Coop answers it.)

COOP :   *(On the phone)* Yes? Oh, hi … Yeah … Yeah. Course I remembered my toothbrush!

FISH: It's his mum.

COOP: I told you, Mum. I'm with Fish and Marko.

FISH: No he ain't, Mrs Cooper! He's with a girl!

COOP: Mum, nothing's going to go wrong!

MARKO: *(In a high voice)* Oo, Cooper! Stop it, please!

(The others laugh. Coop puts his hand over the phone.)

COOP: Shut up, you lot! *(Into phone)* No, it's Marko.

GASMAN: *(High voice)* Oo, Cooper! Have you seen my chop top?

FISH: Crop top, you div!

(Fish and Marko laugh.)

COOP: Shut up! *(Into phone)* What? ... No, I can't call you back, I got no call time left. ... Eh? ... What? Oh ... *(He puts the phone down and swings an arm at Gasman)* You stupid idiot, Gasman!

GASMAN: Wasn't just me!

MARKO: Did you hear him, Coop? Did you hear what he said?

GASMAN: Oh, shut up.

FISH: Chop top! Classic!

COOP: I missed what my mum said through you!

GASMAN: It wasn't just me!

FISH: Careful Coop, he's going to cry again.

MARKO: Yeah, remember last Christmas?

(Gasman puts his hands over his ears.)

FISH: *(Imitating Gasman in tearful voice)* 'I'm sorry I'm late, miss, but I just buried my cat.'

(The others fall about laughing.)

GASMAN: It isn't funny!

(The others laugh even more.)

MARKO: *(Still in Gasman's voice)* He bit through the Christmas lights!

(More laughter.)

GASMAN: *(Intense)* It ain't funny!

COOP: No, you're right, Gasman. Nothing funny about frying your cat.

(More laughter.)

FISH: World's first flying cat – PEEEEOWWWWWW!

(Gasman storms out.)

COOP: Stupid idiot!

FISH: Can breathe again now.

MARKO: Bit mean though, wasn't it?

COOP: Deserved it.

MARKO: He ain't that bad.

(Pause. Fish switches on the video camera.)

FISH: Tension is mounting. Gasman is the first to crack. Fish, Coop and Marko hold firm. The first sighting cannot be far away. *(He switches off the camera.)*

MARKO: I'm hungry.

COOP: As usual.

FISH: Eh, better watch your Sugar Puffs. Gasman's looking for revenge.

MARKO: He'd better not touch my Sugar Puffs.

COOP: He's polishing them off right now.

(Pause.)

MARKO: Just going to check. *(He climbs out of the tent.)*

COOP: *(Laughs)* That got him!

FISH: Lots of room now. *(Pause)* Do you reckon something did touch Gasman?

COOP: Nah. He was just mucking about.

FISH: Didn't sound like he was mucking about.

(Pause. Suddenly Marko crashes back in.)

FISH: What's up?

MARKO: The tent's empty!

COOP: He's gone home!

MARKO: What, and left all his stuff?

FISH: Then, where is he?

MARKO: You tell me, Fish. You tell me.

(The boys look anxiously at one another. Blackout.)

S C E N E T W O

A short time later. It is now completely dark. Fish, Coop and Marko are wandering separately about the field looking for Gasman.

FISH: Gasman! Gasman, you div!

COOP: Come on, Gasman! We were only mucking about.

              (Fish and Coop meet.)

FISH: Any sign?

COOP: Nothing.

              (Fish wheels round.)

FISH: Who's that?!

              (Marko appears, and switches on his torch.)

MARKO: Only me.

FISH: Seen anything?

MARKO: Nope.

COOP: Anyone looked over the cliff?

FISH: Oh, come on!

COOP: You don't know!

MARKO: We shouldn't have picked on him.

FISH: It was nothing.

MARKO: Nothing to you, maybe. You know what happened to that kid at Abbey Park.

FISH: He was bullied.

MARKO: Yeah, like we bully Gasman.

FISH: That ain't bullying!

MARKO: Yeah, not to you, maybe!

FISH: Nah. There's got to be some other explanation.

COOP: Maybe he's in the barn!

FISH: Are you joking? Gasman wouldn't go near that barn!

COOP: We ought to look.

FISH: Yeah, you first.

COOP: No way. This was all your idea.

FISH: I'll go in there. When she's come out.

COOP: There ain't really no ghost!

FISH: Well, you go in, then!

(Pause.)

COOP: I'm cold.

MARKO: I'm hungry.

FISH: You two wouldn't get far in the army.

COOP: We're not in the army! This is supposed to be a holiday!

MARKO: Let's go back to the tents for a bit.

FISH: Tss! Come on then, girls.

(They wander back towards the tents.)

MARKO: Where are they, anyway?

COOP: Just over there, weren't they?

(They look frantically.)

FISH: They're gone!

COOP: They can't be!

FISH: Look! There's our stuff!

(They hurry to where their stuff is scattered.)

COOP: I don't believe this!

FISH: Look, here's the video, just lying here!

MARKO: Do you think Gasman did it?

FISH: Of course Gasman did it!

MARKO: We don't know that.

FISH: *(Sarcastic)* 'We don't know that.' 'We don't know that.' Course we know it! His stuff's all gone!

MARKO: Don't get on at me!

FISH: I'm not getting on at you!

COOP: No, cos Marko didn't organise this, did he, Fish?

FISH: What do you mean? It was Gasman's idea!

COOP: Yeah, but you organised it!

FISH: Least I do something! Least I don't spend my whole life on a stupid Playstation!

COOP: What, are you talking about me?

MARKO: Look, shut up, both of you! This ain't getting us anywhere.

(Fish squats, followed by the others.)

FISH: We're going to freeze if we stay here.

COOP: Too late to get home.

MARKO: Ring your mum.

COOP: I told you! No call time left! She's going to kill me if she finds out about this!

FISH: Maybe we could build a fire.

MARKO: Yeah, come on – let's do that.

(They go about collecting wood, and build a fire.)

FISH: Survivors. That's us.

MARKO: Bet Gasman thought we'd just cave in.

FISH: No chance. Here, tell us another joke, Marko.

MARKO: What do you call a man with a car on his head?

FISH: Go on.

MARKO: Jack.

(The others laugh.)

FISH: That's a wicked one, that.

COOP: I'm starting to enjoy this, in a funny way.

(They finish building the fire.)

MARKO: Right. Who's got the matches?

FISH: Ain't you got them?

MARKO: No.

COOP: I ain't got any.

FISH: Great.

MARKO: We could rub two sticks.

COOP: Oh, sure!

FISH: Did I just feel a spot of rain?

(Pause.)

MARKO: Yeah, it's spitting.

COOP: Aw, no. That's the final straw, that is.

FISH: Quick – get the stuff covered up.

MARKO: What with?

FISH: The sleeping bags.

COOP: Get off! The sleeping bags are the most important things!

FISH: Get lost! I've got a five-hundred quid camera!

COOP: We can't sleep in it, can we?

MARKO: Rain's getting heavier.

FISH: We've got to shelter.

COOP: Oh yeah? Where?

MARKO: Where do you think?

COOP: Oh no. I ain't going in that barn.

          (Blackout.)

Scene Three

Inside the Red Barn. Pitch darkness. Fish stumbles in, carrying his belongings.

FISH: Come on, Coop, you chicken!

(Coop comes inside, also carrying his stuff.)

COOP: My mum's going to kill me.

FISH: *I'm* going to kill you if you don't shut up.

(Marko enters.)

MARKO: It's pitch black.

FISH: Can't you get that torch to work?

MARKO: *(Shaking his torch)* I think the bulb's gone.

FISH: Hand us that plank.

(Coop hands Fish a plank which he uses to jam the door shut.)

COOP: What good's that going to do?

FISH: It's blocking the door, stupid!

COOP: It's not going to stop ... you know.

FISH: 'You know' ain't here. Can you see her?

MARKO: Can't see anything.

COOP: There's a cold breeze coming from somewhere.

FISH: It's called the door.

COOP: No! From inside! Can't you feel it?

FISH: No.

MARKO: There's a bad aura in here.

FISH: *(In a hippy voice)* Bad aura, man.

COOP: You should move that plank. What if we want to get out?

FISH: No!

(Pause.)

MARKO: I just can't see anything!

FISH: Let's sit down here.

(Fish sits, followed by the others. Marko fiddles with the torch. Suddenly a light flashes on.)

COOP: What was that?

MARKO: Dunno!

FISH: It was the torch, stupid!

MARKO: Was it?

FISH: You got a bad connection?

COOP: No, the light came from over there! *(He points.)*

FISH: It did not!

MARKO: *(Bangs torch)* See? Dead.

COOP: Something's in here.

FISH: Rubbish!

COOP: Ssh! *(Pause. The sound of whispering)* Something's rustling.

FISH: Rats.

(Pause.)

MARKO: *(Calls quietly)* Gasman?

FISH: He ain't in here!

MARKO: Ssh! *(Pause)* Gasman?

COOP: Gasman, we know you're in here, so you can come out now!

FISH: *(Swings arm about)* Yeah, come and get a battering!

MARKO: Shut up!

FISH: Oo, what's that smell? Smells like fried cat!

COOP: Bit through the Christmas lights! *(Laughs.)*

MARKO: Shut up! What's the matter with you? It wasn't funny in the first place!

FISH: You laughed.

MARKO: Well, I ain't laughing now!

COOP: Ssh! There's that noise again!

MARKO: *(Checking his luminous watch. He gasps)* Look at the time!

FISH: What?

MARKO: It's midnight, man! It's her time!

FISH: Oh yeah?

(A sudden thump. Fish jumps a mile.)

COOP: The door!

(They freeze. More hard thumps at the door. The plank starts to give way.)

FISH: Where's the mallet?

MARKO: Gasman took it!

COOP: Help! It's her! It's Lady Jasper!

(The door crashes open. The shadowy figure of a woman appears.)

FISH: It's her!

MARKO: *(Prays)* Holy Mary, Mother of God ...

COOP: We're sorry ... we're sorry ... we're sorry ...

VOICE: Is that you, Wesley?

COOP: Mum?

VOICE: Wesley! There you are! I've been worried sick about you! I thought you were supposed to be camping in the field!

(The woman comes closer. She is wearing a headscarf. Her face remains in shadow.)

VOICE: Look, I told you to take a warm jumper, then I find it in your room under your bed! *(Pause)* Whatever's the matter with you all?

FISH: Nothing, Mrs Cooper.

MARKO: Just got a bit ... cold.

VOICE: You look scared, Marko.

MARKO: No, no, I'm fine.

VOICE: What a bunch of lost lambs! Never mind, I'm here now. You're safe with me.

(The lads begin to relax.)

FISH: It's been a weird night, Mrs Cooper.

COOP: We been waiting for a ghost, Mum!

VOICE: A ghost?

COOP: Yeah, Lady Jasper! She like, glows all over, and if she touches you, you've had it!

MARKO: You become one of them!

FISH: The undead!

COOP: Except you ain't really, cos it's just a stupid story.

FISH: And anyway, if the ghost had come, we'd have battered it!

COOP: Yeah, flattened it!

MARKO: Knocked ten bells out of it!

FISH: Yeah, come and get us if you dare, ghostie!

VOICE: As you wish, boys. *(Instant lighting change. The woman rips off her headscarf to reveal Gasman. He has become one of the undead. His face glows a ghostly green.)*

ALL: *(Horrified)* No!

GASMAN: Remember me, boys? Not going to cry, are you?
Not scared of meeting one of the undead?
How about *becoming* one of the undead?
(Gasman advances towards them, arms outstretched.)

ALL: Aaargh! *(They remain frozen to the spot in terror as Gasman reaches towards them. Blackout.)*